FAVORITE BASKETBALL TEAMS

Cleveland Cavaliers

BY ELLEN LABRECQUE

The Child's World®

THE CHILD'S WORLD®
1980 Lookout Drive • Mankato, MN 56003-1705
800-599-READ • www.childsworld.com

ACKNOWLEDGMENTS
The Child's World®: Mary Berendes, Publishing Director
Shoreline Publishing Group, LLC: James Buckley, Jr., Production Director
The Design Lab: Kathleen Petelinsek, Design; Gregory Lindholm, Page Production

PHOTOS
Cover and interior photos: AP/Wide World

LIBRARY OF CONGRESS
CATALOGING-IN-PUBLICATION DATA
Labrecque, Ellen.
  Cleveland Cavaliers / by Ellen Labrecque.
    p. cm. — (Favorite basketball teams)
  Includes bibliographical references and index.
  ISBN 978-1-60253-306-6 (library bound : alk. paper)
  1. Cleveland Cavaliers (Basketball team)—Juvenile literature.
  2. Basketball—Ohio—Cleveland—Juvenile literature. I. Title.
  II. Series.
  GV885.52.C57L33 2009
  796.323'640977132—dc22   2009009787

Printed in the United States of America
Mankato, Minnesota
December, 2009
PA02038

Table of Contents

Go, Cavaliers!

The Cavaliers are one of the most exciting NBA teams to watch. Why? Their star player is LeBron James. LeBron's nickname is King James. He rules the NBA with his awesome game! James led Cleveland to the **NBA Finals** in 2007. He's ready to do it again! Are the "Cavs" your favorite team? Let's meet the Cleveland Cavaliers!

Look out below! Here comes LeBron James for another big slam dunk!

Daniel Gibson isn't afraid to go to the hoop against bigger players.

Who Are the Cavaliers?

The Cleveland Cavaliers play in the National Basketball Association (NBA). The Cavaliers are sometimes called the "Cavs" for short. They are one of 30 teams in the NBA. The NBA includes the Eastern Conference and the Western Conference. The Cavs play in the Central Division of the Eastern Conference. The Eastern Conference Champion plays the Western Conference Champion in the **NBA Finals.**

Where They Came From

The Cavs started playing in 1970. "Cavalier" is a French word for a knight. The Cavaliers are actually the third pro basketball team to play in Cleveland. The Cleveland Rebels played in the Basketball Association of America (BAA) for one season (1946–1947). The Cleveland Pipers later played in the American Basketball League (ABL), also for just one season (1961–1962). The Cavaliers, however, have stuck around for good!

9

Cleveland played Boston in this 1976 NBA playoff game.

Now that LeBron James is on board, the Cavs expect to beat the Bulls.

Who They Play

The Cavs play 82 games from October to April. They play every other NBA team at least once. But when the Cavs play the Chicago Bulls, look out! The game is sure to be a tough battle. The two teams have faced each other five times in the playoffs. The Bulls have won every time. But the Cavs have come close. In fact, in both 1988 and 1989, the Bulls needed all five playoff games to beat them.

Where They Play

The Cavs have played in three different arenas since 1970. Since 1994, they have played in the Quicken Loans Arena. It is nicknamed the "Q." The Q is part of a giant sports and entertainment area. The baseball field for the Cleveland Indians is right next door. LeBron James even attended a playoff game at the baseball field in 2007. But LeBron wore a New York Yankees hat! The Indians still beat the Yankees, 12–3.

13

Cleveland's home in the "Q" is one of the loudest in the NBA.

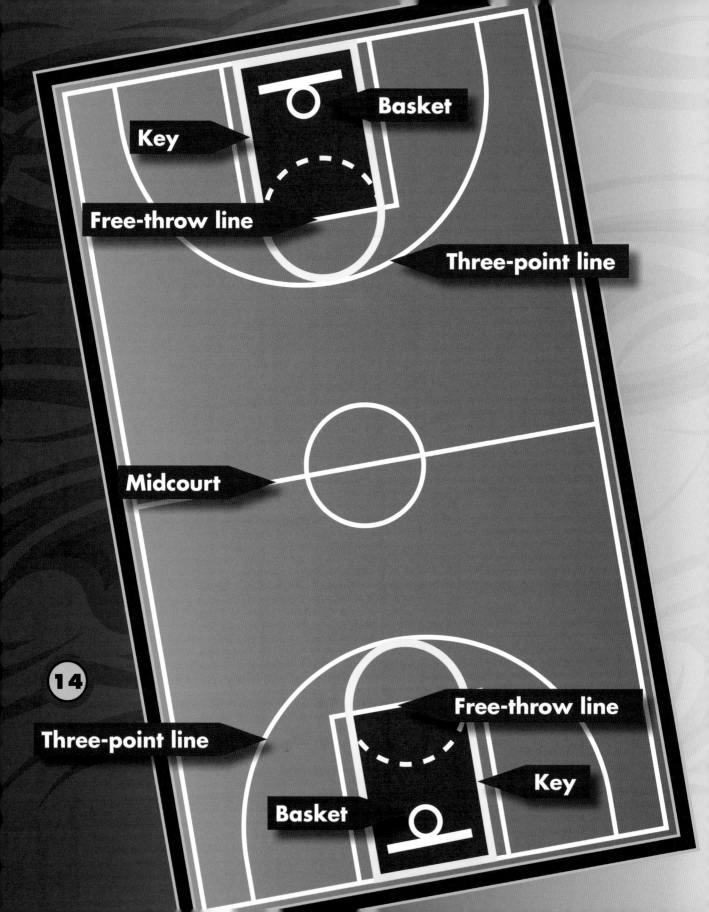

Basket

Key

Free-throw line

Three-point line

Midcourt

Free-throw line

Three-point line

Key

Basket

The Basketball Court

Basketball is played on a court made of
wood. An NBA court is 94 feet (29 m) long.
A painted line shows the middle of the court.
Other lines lay out the free-throw area. The
space below each basket is known as the
"key." The baskets at each end are 10 feet
(3 m) off the ground. The metal rims of the
baskets stick out over the court. Nylon nets
hang from the rims.

Big Days!

The Cleveland Cavaliers have come on strong in recent years—especially since they got LeBron James! Here are three of their greatest moments:

1992: The Cavs advanced to the Eastern Conference playoffs for the first time. In the second round, they beat the Boston Celtics in Game 7, 122–104.

2004: The Cavs doubled their wins from the previous season. LeBron James was named the NBA Rookie of the Year. He is the only Cav ever to receive this honor.

2007: The Cavs made it to the NBA Finals for the first time.

LeBron James starts every game by saluting the Cleveland fans.

17

18

The 2003 season was a long, hard road for the Cavaliers.

Tough Days!

The Cavs have survived plenty of tough times. Here are some of the worst seasons in their history:

1970: In their first season, Cleveland won only 15 games. That was the seventh worst record in NBA history.

1982: The Cavs finished in last place in the league. For a second time, they won only 15 games.

2003: The Cavs wound up winning only 16 games and losing 65. They also failed to make the playoffs for the fifth straight season.

Meet the Fans

Don't mess with Cleveland fans! They're super loyal, and they love the Cavs. Their love and support means that opponents hate to play in Cleveland. In the 2008–2009 NBA season, the Cavaliers lost only two home games! Their record of 39 wins and only 2 losses at home was the second-best in NBA history. With a home record like that, Cleveland is a scary place for anyone playing the Cavs!

STAND UP,

LET'S GO
18-0
CavFanatics!

CAVALIERS
CLEVELAND

Alltel

Cavaliers fans help make their team very hard to beat at home.

Here's Austin Carr in action, dribbling around his opponent.

Heroes Then...

Austin Carr's nickname is "Mr. Cavalier." Carr was a sweet-shooting **guard** who played for Cleveland from 1971 to 1980. **Center** Brad Daugherty was the Cavs' best big man ever. This seven-footer played for the Cavs from 1986 to 1994. During his eight seasons, Brad led the Cavs to the playoffs six times. He also led them in scoring five times. Guard Mark Price played alongside Brad. Price hardly ever missed a shot from the outside. He is the Cavs all-time leader in **three-point shots** made (802).

Heroes Now...

The Cavs today are led by LeBron James. LeBron is faster than most **forwards**. He is stronger than most guards. And he is more skilled than everybody! King James has a court filled with talented teammates. Guard Mo Williams joined the Cavs in 2008. He keeps the Cavs **offense** moving quickly. Ben Wallace is the main man on **defense**. He is also tough and solid—and hard to get around!

Speed and skills made LeBron James the NBA MVP for 2008-2009.

Gearing Up

Cleveland Cavalier players wear a uniform and special basketball sneakers. Some wear other pads to protect themselves. Check out this picture of LeBron James and learn about what NBA players wear.

The Basketball

NBA basketballs are made of leather. Several pieces are held together with rubber edges. Inside the leather ball is a hollow ball of rubber. This is filled with air. The leather is covered with little bumps called "pebbles." The pebbles help players get a good grip on the ball. The basketball used in the Women's National Basketball Association (WNBA) is slightly smaller than the men's basketball.

Headband

Jersey

Wristband

Shorts

Socks

Basketball shoes

This Cleveland jersey uses the team's "classic" logo.

Sports Stats

Note: All numbers shown are through the 2008–2009 season.

HIGH SCORERS

These players have scored the most points for the Cavaliers.

PLAYER	POINTS
LeBron James	12,993
Brad Daugherty	10,389

HELPING HAND

Here are Cleveland's all-time leaders in **assists**.

PLAYER	ASSISTS
Mark Price	4,206
LeBron James	3,159

CLEANING THE BOARDS

Rebounds are a big part of the game. Here are the Cavs' best rebounders.

PLAYER	REBOUNDS
Brad Daugherty	5,227
Zydrunas Ilgauskas	5,069

MOST THREE-POINT SHOTS MADE

Shots taken from behind a line about 23 feet (7 m) from the basket are worth three points. Here are the Cavaliers' best at these long-distance shots.

PLAYER	THREE-POINT SHOTS
Mark Price	802
LeBron James	642

COACH

Who coached the Cavaliers to the most wins?

Lenny Wilkens 316

Glossary

assists passes to teammates that lead directly to making baskets

center a player (usually the tallest on the team) who plays close to the basket

defense when a team doesn't have the ball and is trying to keep the other team from scoring

forwards two tall players who rebound and score near the basket

guard one of two players who set up plays, pass to teammates closer to the basket, and shoot from farther away

NBA Finals the seven-game NBA championship series, in which the champion must win four games

offense when a team has the ball and is trying to score

playoffs a series of games between 16 teams that decide which two teams will play in the NBA Finals

rebounds missed shots that bounce off the backboard or rim and are often grabbed by another player

rookie a new player

slam dunk a shot in which a player stuffs the ball into the basket

three-point shots baskets that earn three points instead of two, because they are shot from behind a line about 23 feet (7.2 m) from the basket

Find Out More

Books

Christopher, Matt. *Greatest Moments in Basketball History.* New York: Little, Brown, 2009.

Craats, Rennay. *Basketball.* Toronto: Weigl Publishers, 2008.

Hareas, John. *Eyewitness Basketball.* New York: DK, 2005.

Jacobs, L. R. *LeBron James: King of the Court.* New York: Grosset and Dunlap, 2009.

Walters, John. *LeBron James.* Mankato, MN: The Child's World, 2007.

Web Sites

Visit our Web page for links about the Cleveland Cavaliers and other NBA teams:

childsworld.com/links

Note to Parents, Teachers, and Librarians: We routinely verify our Web links to make sure they are safe, active sites—so encourage your readers to check them out!

Index

ELLEN LABRECQUE

Ellen Labrecque has written books for young readers on basketball, tennis, ice hockey, and other sports. Ellen used to work for Sports Illustrated Kids magazine and has written about many NBA stars. She likes to watch basketball. The Philadelphia 76ers are her favorite team.